Becoming Mother

poems

Rhonda Elizabeth Nichols

ISBN-13: 978-0-578-78419-9

Editor/Book Design: Ash Good, *ashgood.com*
Cover painting: Brenda Walther, *theraggededge.org*
Author portrait: Brian Geraths, *studiobpdx.com*

Dedicated to my parents:
Kathleen Hilda Bone Paddon, who
inspired me to write my first poem,
and Reginald Francis Paddon,
who will always be my favorite poet.

Preface

This book tells the story of my journey in poems. I have been asked to put them in a collection. These pieces are not in chronological order but appear in a sequence that feels right to me. Thank you for giving witness to my words such as they are.

I want to give a special thank you to those who have mothered and mentored me: Sherry Anderson, Marlene Olson, Joyce Davis, and—the only grandmother I remember—Mabel Paulene Nichols. Their unconditional love and faith carried me through many hours of doubt.

Thank you to Susan Rueling Furness in whose writing workshop I first heard my voice and Brenda Walther for believing my words belong in the world.

I also want to thank my daughters, Carmella and Marlena, for being my greatest teachers who pushed me to grow by testing my love and will.

And a deep gratitude to Curtis, my husband whose steady, unselfish love enabled me to become *Mother*.

~ *Rhonda Elizabeth Nichols*

Poems

III.   A mother's heart catches things that fall before they shatter

VI. She is all of you, and she is me

Becoming Mother

~ I ~

Daughters don't want to be their mothers

In deep fall

leaves remind me
of the beauty of harvest—
late stages of our pilgrimage

we journey

Every beginning has its promise—
fresh purpose, discovery

Through the proving seasons
of spring & summer
we sow—
giving our lives to something

But in deep fall
we reap
the legacy of what we've proved—
what never fell off in the shaking

Is it faith?
Or sheer determination
that makes the last apple hang on
when all others have fallen?

Maybe a late maturing—
only to fully ripen
on that last day
when winter comes for good

❖

These daughters

begin in innocence,
enshrouded in promise
Grow to become
elusive strangers
sharing our household
sparingly, as friendships
test the goodness
of a mother's heart

Daughters
don't want to be their mothers—
flawed, unyielding, permanent

But given trauma,
given storms and heartache,
women circle wagons
certain the wealth of history
will reveal loving bonds
never broken,
tempered fires never quenched

These daughters,
born of our flesh,
unite us with all those
who know—even when strangers
in our very own household

❖

Homeland of My Soul

The call of the Almighty,
a gentle sure hello,
draws out soul living
and shows where to go

It's the realm of spirit teachers
that awes this simple girl
I find family in your comfort
a stranger wouldn't know

Is it hard to hear answers
whispered from our giver?
Does He hold out vision
awaiting our surrender?

Does forever really matter
when we must live today?
Can a broken heart be lifted
when in fragments it lays?

There is this urge inside me
to lay down at your feet
Become a bridge of flesh and shield
you from raging waters, deep

But I can only suffer
inside my own thin shell
while holding treasured trinkets
I fondle and reshelve

New life comes so slowly
Its beauty bloom unfolds
None can hasten the budding
in honest hearts revealed

I have often wondered
where I'd be without you
Just another vagabond
aimlessly wandering

But I know where to go to listen
for waves from a distant shore
A peaceful place within me —
the homeland of my soul

❖

When there's little we can do

Even less we understand,
it's better to leave unsaid
well-meaning words
that stumble out our mouths

I love you,
wrapped in a hug,
does more for heartbreak
than eloquence
without courage to be present

❖

It's no wonder

old women know sacrifice
They've seen the darkness
that grabs babies in adolescence,
forever changing what was normal
to some horrible nightmare
that becomes our life

Why wouldn't we be driven
to soft couches in quiet rooms
where therapists
sit in timed listening?

Pour out pent up shame
that holds us hostage
inside walls of grey
no flower can color

It's a thankless job
few do well,
but we get by
Become mothers
that screw up the next generation
while we try to mend ourselves

❖

The mother in me

tends to see
the amusing ways of her daughters
while left to ponder
this job I've grown into,
amazed I'm even here!

Little arms reach out to hug,
kisses come at me, a cheek I extend
Retching, fevers, puberty and moods
Despair, triumphs and tender looks

Nurture I've longed for, I freely give
and respect their anger, uncertainty and wit
These girls have raised me, born of my womb,
now showing me the delight of a *Heelys* shoe

Their gentle pleading of *sing us to sleep*
settles and calms me, thinking of Thee—
watching these souls tender and new,
working inside them as You're allowed to

Their eyes are on me dancing around the room
while, too loud, the beat escorts in a tune
I'm happy to be here—a mother I've become
The struggles are many, but *oh how I've learned*

My heart is extended and joy is increased
Sorrows divided when shared in grace
There's rest in the heart of a mother's embrace—
advocate, believer in your innocence

❖

I Want

It doesn't interest me
that you have excuses, justifications
for what you are doing
I want what's real—
what motivates your life,
what you see in the darkness

It doesn't interest me
what things you desire
or where you think you are going
I want to know what you feel—
what makes your pulse quicken,
what makes your heart sing

It doesn't interest me
what clothes you wear
or the car you drive
I want to know how you survived—
how you cried through your losses,
kept from setting fire to your past

It doesn't interest me
to know your successes
I won't bore you with mine
I want to hear your poems,
your subtle observations
and profound revelations
that brought depth to your soul

I want to see what makes your eyes shine,
your smile radiate, your step spring
I want the sharing that flows from trust—
deep trust that's seen the bottom of hell
and returned without a hair singed

❖

There are friendships

I hold closely, fervently
Others hang loosely
on the fringes
of my consciousness
where they resurface
when my phone rings

I treasure all of you
who have seen me through
dark valleys of uncertainty
and the horror of grief

Though I've barely lived,
I've read countless faces
Troubled eyes have told me
more than what's been said

Many times I've held my breath,
looked away and obsessed
at what I could not change

My discomfort
almost unmanageable
Yet still I stay
because you foster
new leaves of growth

I'm a wreck in my neurosis
but remain, to those closest,
the friend you've come to know
I've found in my soul
a place just for you

❖

Life is more than we put on FB

Fooling others into jealousy
while we live lives no one would trade for
If they only knew the pain behind the smile,
the lonely hours of uncertainty,
the unrelenting doubts that drive us
to beautiful places for a few photos
we look back on with longing

❖

Under the mango tree

dreams are sprouting
opportunities like summer seeds
opening to growth,
transformation

Here on borrowed money
spent to sow greater promise
Fruitful, like the hanging mangos
decorating an old tree

What will become of the reaping
is anybody's guess
We sow without an answer
Keep coming back in faith

We will reap what we sow
lest we live carelessly
And barren ground longstanding
holds no beauty for the belly

Here under the mango,
someone planted
an orange soft offering
I taste

The long wait over
The sweetness of effort
greets me
like an old friend

❖

Maroota, NSW

Birds of the morning
serenade a new day,
all the night forgotten
by burgeoning sunlight

They sing for one another
while a traveler, alone,
savors contentment
The softness of gratitude
envelops my soul

Given one more journey
to this land of youth dreams,
a sanctuary in my thoughts
from troubles that raged

Travel is . . .

the escape we yearn for
to change our perspective
aright our leanings
and enlarge our heart

I gave myself to dreaming
of the Southern Cross
Stars that bow to ceiling height,
where I befriend their lights

Though vast the universe,
of this I am assured,
the One who brought it all to pass
is still the one who cares

❖

Goodbye's unsaid

breed regret
If I never return

carry me
in the bounty
of your heart

Thankful
for rainbow reflections
in our tears

❖

~ II ~

We don't know until we know

Poetic Justice

They say it takes courage
to leave what's killing you
But do they know heartache?
My trying companion

Will I survive this train wreck?
Will I breathe free?
Will I own the lessons
given to me?

If we live once,
or a thousand times,
hurt feels the same
Scars are living proof
something had to die

It's poetic justice
I knew my sappy heart
would end up shredded
by the risks I took
and depths I mined
for one golden nugget
I had to give back

❖

Blackened Bread

Disappointing even when hidden
under layers of butter and jam

Some things we longed for
are best thrown away

❖

Like a Whisper

I run with wolves,
fly with ravens,
sleep with the homeless
in gutters of this world

I walk with gypsies,
talk with reverends,
hold hands with the broken
in polite circles of honor

I wrestle with doubt—
that pompous bully—
match after match

I light up in poetry,
express emotion
dripping from the lips
of the wronged, eloquent

I live for freedom in my spirit,
unburdened by sorrow or
disappointment,
I beg for the return of contentment
settled in timeless purpose

I've tasted the bitter herbs of change,
defiant in the closing door,
awakening now to new possibility
and the illusion of happily ever after

Don't judge me by my colors,
my stripes or spots
Love me differently
than the usual comforts
of your reality

Let me pass among you
like a whisper
and leave you wondering
what you missed

❖

Old people

are reaping what they've sown
as the body decays and
independence slips away

Their minds dim with worry, regret
Obsess about what's been lost
Can you see it?
Do you feel their angst?

Some rage at their condition—
beg for the Lord's taking
so suffering will end

They want to be in charge of something,
render themselves relevant again
while their offspring hover like vultures
after scraps of money to be left

❖

Arbor Wisdom

We don't know until we know
what will become of us
Years yield to habits
What we embrace,
what we run from,
shaped by health, pain

The unlucky become lucky
because they know
the limitations of existence
and settle into contentment
like those who can't remember
anything anymore

❖

Peace

is the absence of fear—
saying what we mean without judgment

Honesty in an atmosphere of safety—
being who we are without critic or editor

Peace is walking our talk and being secure in it—
believing we are a small part of something divine

Peace is believing we are made for these times—
we are in the right place, right generation

Peace is the result of faith—
something we can't see but feel its effects every day

Peace is knowing ourselves, forgiving ourselves,
accepting compliments and sharing our stories

Peace doesn't come from the outside,
but is found in the deep reaches of the soul

Draws us like a warm fire,
peace is just enough

❖

The stone

tells me we are shaped by time
Constant flow smooths out our rough places
Trees fall like old pillars we've loved,
their weight leaving impressions we carry

We are marked by our experience
and remain in the stream of life ever-changing
Until, chosen by someone with greater purpose,
we're found, plucked up and admired
for the beauty time has created

The stone tells me I matter, always,
and given perfect timing, events unfold
Others are touched
because we are there waiting, ready, open

The stone reminds me of how beautiful old people are
How their lives inspire us, reveal how well they loved
What didn't kill them made them beautiful

The stone's hard surface is almost transparent
like a window inviting me to look deeper
We share revelations that only come in quiet
       contemplation—
sitting at the bedside of someone dying,
counting time in rhythmic breathing until its final sigh

❖

La Provence

Every tree has rings of suffering
that grow beyond the scars
Only those who cut it down
see evidence of hard times

Storms pass through
testing roots and the will
to grow taller, fuller—
to become
what a seed started

Have patience in the journey
People passing through
slip through our hands like pebbles
blending in with others

Their purpose goes uncherished
until they disappear
and we search in desperation
for what we know is lost

❖

The embrace

holds everything
You in your anxiety and sorrow—
a beautiful young mother
prone to darkness
who already lost more than is bearable

You with dark-haired honesty
in a family closer than the rest of us

The embrace started from across the room
I dropped everything to hold you
Tighter
Feeling like nothing else could show you
how my heart breaks

For you, I fear what is coming

How *do* you lose your only sister?
By inches
First the long wavy hair
From poison pumping through shy veins
while she battles a determined enemy

One *good year* is what you asked for
Losing people isn't what we do well
Is it easier to live the trauma
than stand by watching in helpless admiration
as the one you love slips away?

❖

My view

from the lowlands,
rises like fog as the sun
sheds light on the valley

Up is where my help comes
Up is where the canvas spreads,
painted colors more vivid
than the grass beneath

I wait in expectancy
for what I have not known
and what I still must learn

Pen to paper, small and silent
I wrestle with what I love
and what loves me, eternally

And yet, in the lowlands
my steps leave impressions,
each one clumsy but sure

I lean against the oaks
that dotted my childhood,
gently calling, unmovable

Time pushes onward
covering the pain of children
who never mourned a father
that left without goodbye

From the lowlands
Mom sees his heartbeat
still pumping through trenches,
carrying water,
bringing seeds to harvest
and she is pleased

❖

Fallen down

horses with their legs askew are
forced by nature to find a new view
Laid on their backs, look up to the sky
above the dark river that hides all this pride

Haunted and heavy secrets are kept
Joy for the joyless, oh how they've wept
Blessed old children, availed of their charm
hold onto chances of doing us harm

Fall and be broken, alas all is well
To see a new purpose, I cannot tell
Awake to the answers that swim in my head
I go with new gusto where I once walked with dread

These siblings of sisters tighten my gut
I've judged and hurt badly, no knowing what
difficult answers await parenthood
To excuse what is ugly sharpens my mood

Focus and follow, accept what you can
Eyes opened wide to the frailties of man

❖

I reach

for a garment bag that holds my yesterdays,
move through the dusty haze
that complicates my day
and long for some conclusion of all the pain
brought forth—some avenue to forgiveness
deep inside my soul

I'm getting there (or so it seems)
but I've lost my heart somewhere
I sort through the empty days when rage
was all I knew—we matter not, this tribe
of kids—*to whom do we belong?*
I unpack these days behind locked bars
that muted any song

Who can tame the demons rage? The lifeless,
deathless roar of doubt and fear and unbelief
and knowing better now?

Urged to go, we plod along in an endless drone
Where to go but far out there, far from what was home?

I am motherless and full of punk, still
so much to prove
Folks who cared about my soul loved this feisty,
mouthy girl running from a wretched past—
doubtless, time will tell but we know
not what our end will be (or who will pay the bill)

I see you suffer on the way—a bird
with broken wings afraid to fly, but a sitting duck
will be lunch for someone else
Go my daughter—rise and shine—
Ahead are better days
Walking, sober, mystified . . .
How do you love so much?

❖

I wanted to be an artichoke

dipped in mayonnaise,
savored slowly
petal by petal
My thorns requiring you
to hold me gingerly
and take enough time
to get to my heart
Full of feeling,
my tender center
would be welcomed
by determined diners

But my sister
was a cucumber—
juicy, skinny,
a little bitter
about being second
behind a thistle bloom
Today she's tasty, creative,
without children to wonder
if her skin is the shade of green
that needs peeling or not

Mother wanted pickles
and was determined to prepare us
for long term preservation
only to find our dates
past "use by" so threw us out
in favor of little brother,
who came to the table
a perfect potato salad

❖

Long Aqua Board

Do you remember?
Wrinkled toes walking, hesitating
on the long aqua board
fifteen feet above the water

To jump once was a family rite of passage
How you pushed beyond fear, euphoric
as your feet touched air
How it stung your legs and belly
How you proved you weren't a sissy

Do spring buds fear the opening?
Pushed and taunted by jealous branches
until a final explosion of color
as if turned inside out

Yes it hurts to grow
You're never what you used to be
Innocence and ignorance traded away
for burgeoning understanding

You go again
Arms wrapped around your shivering body
Rung after rung, hands up the ladder
Because you see yourself braver now
and your siblings say your name with a spark of awe

❖

A mother's heart catches things that fall before they shatter

Urine

on her roses
made her livid
when they died

Urine
was his weapon—
saying what he couldn't,
doing what he wouldn't

Words inside never escaped
his careful emotions overlaid

Urine
was his bedroom odor
when nothing made sense
and pleasure was smothered
under bland bedsheets

But urine meant he was alive—
still my father—
until the color darkened kidneys
gave up trying

I saw him fevered and small,
patched with morphine
Those last hours we sang as children
around a bed,
accepting that he could hear us
even if no hand would squeeze back
so we could be sure

❖

You died while

I slept in peace
on the other side of town
Your last breath ebbed
wrapped in a daughter's embrace
She loved you more
than any other on earth

Our moment in private—
your eyes rolled back
I groped for words
knowing they were my last
You're going home, Poppa
It's coming real soon
This one-sided conversation bound me—
your mouth open, breathing ragged

I came to sing you off to sleep,
my heart bursting from me
Unwavering notes of assurance
my vital, tender final gift

In your pale, feverish fetal pose
quivering lips sucked at the sponge
Too much moisture, panicked eyes
trying to cough from deep inside

Her hands caressed your chest
calming in comfort, reassuring
while near your bedside Steve scrambled
for a morphine patch on your skin

We are witnesses to a solitary journey,
awaiting heaven's taking
The call came in my morning haze
Elated to hear your suffering ended

I arrived again at your bedside
You, lifeless, eyes closed by another
Your body still warm to my touch
Stuffed dog placed at your head

Your form lingers while in other rooms
people laugh, remember and make plans
I am the only one bothered?
Do our lives just move on
while a dead man sleeps?

❖

Sweet Endings

As I sit and ponder remaining days in doubt
amazed at God's goodness and how it's worked out
my heart is much softer, the chains of the past
have broken and freed me to hold nothing back

To grieve my dear Poppa, grateful for him,
his order and patience for this ending to come
I stand here sober, soaked to the bone
God's love poured upon me, can't take it all in

But nothing is wasted, affects others too
the beautiful people, my friends who knew
Come drought or bounty God meant them to be
a tender reminder He's thinking of me

Alone in my grieving, He only knows
the sorrow and beauty of souls going home
I'll miss my sweet Poppa but in me I see
the incredible treasure he passed on to me

His spirit of kindness, his faith in the tree
Calvary made ready our way to be free
So much forgiveness, not something forced
but in God's time perfect, helps bring it about

I'm grateful for freedom deep in my soul
The fighting is over I'm closing that door
Understanding brings wisdom, hope conquers all
Charity is balm for my grieving heart

Thank you, sweet Jesus, for the impossible dream—
a mother and father in love at the end
Carry my sorrow with tears freely shed
This small human vessel needs to expand

So little I'm holding, let it change me the more
Let it inspire others to put faith in your will

❖

Loss

Thankfulness is what happens
when love trumps fear
Eyeball to eyeball with grief
we surrender to change

Walking through fires of naked emotion
our next breath is never certain
Hug tightly, love deeply
Loss might be the only teacher we learn from

❖

I come from

words, emotion,
Welsh singers and strong women
who love with food and garden

I come from sunny skies, poison oak,
batting rocks, walking on fences,
From butter churns and marble players

I come from a wooden hoop,
boysenberry pies, apricot trees
From bee stings and pulling weeds

I come from playground fights, bicycle pedals,
hot lunches with tin foil covers
From many dishes and laundry piles

I come from country roads, garbage dumps,
deer crossings, steelhead runs
From stranded sheep and trimming hooves

I am the childhood I loathed
sweetened by time and perspective

My untold story
found in the pages I keep

❖

Fraggleding

He is more than a number
His place in the family line is nine
The first of the second family
(though we're supposed to be one)

He was a fraggleding
The best kind to grow up with
Creative and bold
blazing his own trail

A fraggleding pushes things up and open
ever curious about lardo and bull snizzle
He would beckon for me to follow
and I would, before finding myself in an awful
frackle!

Sour and moody from the sky falling parental
kerfuffle
we'd both retreat to scheming of another adventure

It might have been the butt quacks
that started our side-splitting guffaws
while on the road with too many related humans

It was a lockdown sort of drive
with warnings of a thin belt spanking
or *come here so I can give you a pinch*

Fraggledings are noisy and feisty
which is hard on whoever's driving
especially Dad

❖

I wish I knew

what dogs dream about,
what old men regret,
what mothers never lose

I wish I knew how time robs us
of strength and mind but not spirit

I wish I knew my mother's first husband
His death changed everything

I wish I knew joy unaffected by circumstance
Embracing the deep work of sorrow
Black lines enhancing the colors of my life

❖

The tangled web of feelings

time unwinds—
a childhood some never get over,
running from the shame
and scars of loneliness

Heaven forbid
I repeat the struggle,
passing on
the black cloud of unhappy

We relive the torment
when our children pass
from toddlers
on to hair-raising adolescents

I find myself
in water over my head

Show me
a place of acceptance
lest old wounds reopen
and I taint my offspring
with jaded bits of sarcasm
and stony unforgiveness

❖

The Process Growing Requires

The softness of a mother's heart
catches things that fall before they shatter
but can the dreams we've hatched
find their wings?
Stretch enough, try enough
to catch the winds of promise?

Where is my patience or my faith
as I watch the cracking of the egg?
Little beak emerges as you show yourself
and hints of what you will become

Stop me from peeling back the shell
in my eagerness to "help"

Keep my hands away
from the process growing requires

Let me not pollute the purity of your discovery
Let your life be its own expression
of creativity and hope

Don't mar your thirst to live
with excuse or reservation
There are no challenges too great
no roads too steep, or rivers too wide
when you trust your soul

Let it lead you through every valley
over every mountain
Be reminded it's the journey
rich with experience that fulfills

I am still learning
beauty is in authenticity and the courage
to be ourselves without exception—
to allow myself to be the mother that I am

❖

Children

Water
running over
dams held so long—
cracked
frayed

The damage grows
and there's no going back
to innocence

Children
are fickle

No telling how futile
our attempts at teaching
integrity

Those who are drawn to fire
will burn
in flames of desire
and willfulness

Who accepts
this great responsibility
of soul's lent
and the care of them?

Only desperate prayer
keeps me
from running off a cliff

Escaping
this thing I've chosen
in the confidence of youth
when I knew everything
and pompously told you so

❖

It's the muddle of motherhood

we love and loathe
in this dicey earth dance
between guilt and joy

The job is timeless—
once you're in
you never get out
Only death releases
the grip of heartache, hope
and teeth grinding worry
that swallows rational thought

Motherhood is complicated
by layers of emotion
and ancient expectations
that echo in our emptying brains

How to ever be good enough
in our own mind
when our peers heap admiration
on what we can not escape

We choose to marry
Choose motherhood
believing we will do a better job
than all those we criticized
in our youth

Well guess what?!
Motherhood is a muddle—
an upside down all out
fist fight of a struggle
we endure (and most survive)

Bring me the words
that ping pong in your head
Speak out loud the shameful intentions
that crush your heart
Hold open arms
for hugs from afar

Through the lifelong learning
that makes old women
so gracious to behold,
we'll get there sweet mothers

❖

~ IV ~

Pushing is what we do

Pushing

slender, green bodies upward,
purchased and planted with expectation

Pushing is what we do

Releasing children from warmth and water
into the blinding lights of brick and mortar
because we want to see them
and it's time for pushing when there's no room left

Skin stretched beyond proper measures
and I am grumpy anyway
Following the DNA of our mothers
who taught us to mistrust the widening hips,
who chased the maiden's mystique
with bottles of dye, gyms and ignored birthdays

We want to live forever
until we don't

Time casting a shadow
on grand illusions and broken promises

But the daffodils don't seem to mind
They push because it's time to appear in bowed
heads of yellow,
humbled by this journey from darkness into light,
and stun the winter landscape with their offering

❖

New is not old

not second, not last
New is beginning
A fresh start
full of hope and renewal

New is gracious, forgiving
Turning from the bondage of what was
and never again will be

New is open to possibilities
It's right on and enduring
New will see things differently
changed and observing

New is the day of birds
singing ancient melodies
for fresh ears
New generations of people
passing through turbulent waters
where families tend to capsize

Old people leave fading impressions
we savor then forget

We too will pass into oblivion
aged and bent over from neglect
Time heals the heartaches
once felt keenly in my chest

Wounded by unsuspecting children
making their way out of the nest
I go, believing new is necessary
this time new is best

❖

My daughter, my love

wants me to write
lines of compliment
lines of connection
absent in the drowning
lines of darkness
that color adolescence

We blame ourselves
We blame our parents
We shoulder our friends
like we're their mothers

Forgotten in the struggle
is the breath we breathe
the words we think
and constant distraction
of moving pictures, moving apps

Gobbling up time
like it's not precious
ignoring the milestones
that make up childhood

Afraid of growing up
Sneaking chocolates to soothe
the lonely wounds of a sister
who took everything
by coming first,
shadowed by the fear
those with chronic illness know

Are we not all broken
by the long suffering it takes
to grow from a child into adulthood?
Are there no memories of wonder?
No playback or rewind

Our lives are a vapor rising
on a warming field
Too soon the sun erases
its faint whisper,
leaves only the hot rays of midlife
and exposes the consequences
of ignorance and illusion

Difficulties remind us to feel
Learn contentment with what is
or let the need to be comfortable
drive us toward the life we want

❖

Graduation

for Carmella

I didn't know
when you entered our life
how my heart would grow
through the struggle and strife

It takes a village someone said
to dispel the critic in your head
The perfect parent I'll never be,
but I am the mother I wanted for me

Eighteen years to get it right:
Hug like you mean it
Have a good cry
Eat your veggies
Get more sleep
Be kind to yourself
Skip over puddles
and choose the deep

Don't despair,
you will find those like you
and when you do . . .
keep them
and they will keep you

❖

Cocoon

Bits of papered history
behind cabinet doors

Your childhood journey
left for me to store

Oh such brilliance!
Such a heart of gold!

Skin of adolescence
shed for unfolding wings

I gently finger
the shell of your cocoon

Mother tears fall softly
but with no regret

Given a gift so precious,
awed by time's quick flight

❖

Tribe of Poets

I follow
the hard pits
inside ripened fruit
that show up
expectedly
when sweetness subsides
and we're left wanting
what's already gone

I roll them around
inside my mouth
remembering

I'll never be a polished poet—
there's too much raw

But I'll feel all things
like the tribe of poets
to which I belong

❖

So Much of any Year is Flammable

Grocery lists, statements, gas receipts
Soon all will be paperless
How sad to miss the scribbled lines
so perfectly said, from inspired hearts
or signatures in hasty ink
casually revealing personality

My father practiced penmanship
on the backs of envelopes
His primary teacher
still over his shoulder at seventy-five

So much of that year forgotten
All tossed aside except impressions
which never fade or lose their fire
when you're a daughter

❖

Sifting

through relics of a childhood gone—
confessions of love
on teacher-directed Mother's Day cards
remind me of simpler times

We are many of one mother
carving out our scattered lives
clutching memories
as the last known home is disassembled

I feel sadness at her walls
that echo empty
This was a place of miracles
last breath, last goodbyes

It's the end of an era

Let me welcome the sorrow
and remember how short
one breath, one life

❖

Settling

Leaving
is believing
accepting
what your heart
already knows

Settling
for a life half lived
doesn't guarantee
peace

But settling
is what we do
because dying embers
are safer
than raging infernos

❖

Rebuild

on gratitude and the freedom
love extends
to be ourselves again
In the quiet of acceptance
choices made beyond my vision

Hand in hand in a circle grieving,
invited to howl at the moon,
it feels authentic and appropriate
to raise our voices of sorrow
in unison as candles flicker

Just as sitting in the
backroom of Barbacoa
with good food and ambiance —
some things are right
and only you know it

If I'm a reminder of the past
let it be a time of gratitude
that lingers in your memory
Not a sharp exchange of regret
or an unyielding heart of resistance

I don't need the limelight,
embellishment or half-truths
Only the simplicity of knowing
I mattered when things were tough—
that I gave what I could

Released from chains of expectation
and the harsh aftermath of longing
that would accompany separation,
rebuild with more substance than flare
I want freedom to dwell in my body

❖

Marmalade & Tea

If I could see
through the eyes of forgiveness
the future would call
in beckoning echoes

I'd serve toast for breakfast
with marmalade and tea
like an English dignitary
across the open sea

I risk nothing by going onward
glad for passing time
and its ability to soften
the misery of youth

Time is cloaked in kindness
for those who carry on
Let the dead be buried
with their demons and scars

I relish their passing wisdom
left on the lips of children
who carry themselves
in strong family resemblance

I am not free of offenses
but choose compassion
as my nightly confidante—
one who listens without speaking
and nods in understanding
being the old sage that she is

❖

Healing

begins
when
in patience
we sit with ourselves
long enough
to love
nurture
and accept
what the mirror
reflects

❖

These Times

On the deserted streets of yesterday
lie broken promises of prosperity

People try to make sense
of what happened to their livelihood,
falling into arms of family
shedding selfish ambitions
and return to community

How can we bewail these times
unless we remain looking back
at what we thought we had?

It's the artists, poets penniless
who own the golden goose
A creative well that produces
regardless of circumstance

Why do we stagger at today?
Why not see what the rats see?
Do what eagles do
following their God-given instinct?
To live and enjoy
in the limitations of their kind

We are not meant for glory
but to reflect God's perfection
in the flaws of man

❖

~ V ~

I am thankful that motherhood is hard

Embarking on a New Adventure

Father guide my little ship
May it glide through calmer waters
than the seasoned mast and slip

I look toward a red horizon
sure of beauty to behold
So much unseen living under,
let the waves of faith unfold

Little ships are made to weather
all the mighty storms alone
when at the helm a Guide far wiser
shows the way with distant stars

I am a weary seaborne traveler
But still, I seek another soul
Will my days add to the treasure
I've carried long and still hold close?

❖

New Year

Time
is the luxury
we can't afford
to waste

Heal well
O' nation

Heal well
dear one

Rise, be going
No bridges burning
No empty yearning
for what's behind

Keep close the memory
of those you lost
Be kinder, stronger
in the shoes they left

A new beginning
invites
our gratitude,
our grace

❖

Deliberate Perseverance

There's a line
on every horizon
Beyond it:
unknown

Before it, all is seen,
a blur or fine detail

What I feel
affects the scenery,
my view skewed
by muddy banks of a pit
or stunning vistas
from hard-earned summits

I choose
the hands I hold,
sticks to harm or support
My integrity proved, exposed
A window of what's inside

If the answers are within me,
may the clogged pipes
find air and light again

❖

You Speck of Dust

Time slips through the hourglass
Each grain of sand falls
on the lines of our face
When will that last grain drop?

It's not my place to shout eloquence
in the streets of shame
but to see the good in every eyelash,
each perfect petal,
fingering stones
shaped by timeless waters

I'm not the one with answers
but one voice to ask aloud
why these times seem different?
Clouds of fear permeate—
a culture clutching guns
worships traceable gadgets
bombarding our minds
with toxic information—
cause the forgetful to pray
when nothing else brings comfort

How have we become immune
to the dignity of listening,
to the host of all creation
whose beauty we covet
in our lives and sacred spaces?

He's waiting for us, calling to us
Come and rest
Settle down, you speck of dust
Everything that matters
is bigger than this

Galt, Calif.

I can skim the surface
for pieces of debris
with a long poled net
in a man-made oasis

Or take a long dive inward
without oxygen tanks
looking for lost treasure

Bits of my experience
lay at the bottom
unchanged by time
or the cloak of murky waters

Treasure I have forgotten
removed from their purpose
by layers of life
I wrestle with that
with what times does to me

I can lie in green pastures
without trying to devour
every blade of grass

I can rest content now
knowing I will again
feel the angst of deep despair
as part of my human condition

We can live in the whirlwind
of a dying, fearful society
without the madness
that drives people to extremes

Because peace doesn't come
from the outside
but the inner being of my solitude
and the more I dwell there
I remember
I am a pilgrim passing through

❖

So Concludes Another Year

A collection of fleeting stories,
some pages tearstained,
some pages dog-eared
for one more quick read

Love is the ink that flows
unrelenting
before time reveals
the last punctuation

❖

Thursdays

I laughed with her
when we couldn't cry—
it was always out loud

Her disease robbed her of words
I could hear what she was saying in her eyes
When she knew, I knew, we laughed out loud

A mixture of relief and joy
to feel understood, accepted
after another week of frustration
and puzzlement among her peers

They knew her when she could talk well
and saw her decline with pity

That spontaneous laughter was beautiful
Her childlike wonder magical
I saw in her the true woman—flawed
but real and fiercely independent

She has moved on but left me
with a remnant of her story
in an ancient shark's tooth
that she wore daily

A sharp reminder of who she always was inside

❖

Bits in the Sky

Today is the day after
A day without expectations
Without the weight of before
that brought guilt, anxiety

Yesterday I watched cranes—
only visitors here—
take a restful stop
along their journey

These cranes are fleeting
as are mothers, who
bent over with age
elicit more compassion

Gone is the rage of youthful indignation
and the sour taste of impossibility

Up and away
winged wonders take to the sky—
passing as all things do

Only in their leaving
do we comprehend
their gift

❖

Bataclan Theater

I think of you
in long stretches of silence

You who witnessed them dying
in loving exchanges

You who played dead
as vultures circled,
guns aimed at any movement

You said it's the cries of grown men
holding dead girlfriends
that haunt you

Part of you died with them
in the Bataclan carnage

Are the dead more fortunate
to remember no more
those awful moments
before life drained out
from bullet wounds that
shattered youthful flesh?

We are left in stunned revulsion
at the utter callousness
of this massacre

A war waged against
the sick ideals of poverty
and an unknown god
that promises lies
to those willing to kill for them

❖

El Niño

Give me water
cool and clean
from the grey of December
where rising rivers
help me remember

A yesteryear
when sandbags and plywood
held back the Willamette
and you were born
while the Dogwood bloomed

Give me water
stashed on mountain peaks
cooling streams of summer
growing dreams and daughters
in this place I call home

❖

Transition

I reach for his skin
twenty-five years familiar

Skin washed in tears
of my frustration

Skin that holds my secrets
without demand or judgment

A sudden surge of summer
breaks within me

I fling off the sheets
and distance myself in a pool of sweat

I'm sorry I say feeling betrayed
by this body retreating back to girlhood

You may laugh or cry
scream or sigh

but there's no escaping
a woman in transition

❖

I am thankful

that motherhood is hard
that being kind is always right
and that I am surrounded by people who grow

Joy comes from investing my heart—
this is always true
even when heartbreak is guaranteed

❖

Mina

I cradled you
in youthful arms—
a novice at motherhood

You were second
and still no manual appeared

You were a baby
when diabetes came knocking
and I cried
for your sister and us

You were neglected some,
when blood sugar lows,
shots and guilt
left you wondering
where mother had gone

How unfair the attention
a little girl sees—
we favored your sister
to keep her alive

Lost in the shuffle
you wandered alone
but through the fire
you rose

A beautiful soul—
kinder, sweeter
than I deserved
Now a woman
trying new wings

I love you
for the journey
you never betrayed

A chapter ending
A new one begins

Go, my daughter,
in virtue, in wonder
Step out in your skin
while I stay behind

❖

~ VI ~

She is all of of you, and she is me

Lake Audy, MB

I walk with you
hand in hand
across the fields
of familial land

I feel your sorrow
and despair
I see this place,
what brought you here

A tragic end
we cannot change,
a father's voice
never heard again

From far away
I study maps,
wish some way
to touch your face

Taste the cold,
give you warmth,
hold your heart
in silence

Beautiful child,
all grown up,
you somehow knew
this would be

And so it is—
God takes
God gives

Open-hearted,
always loved

❖

Dear Dad,

is it okay that I miss you?
Silver hair, watery eyes
Your road wasn't easy but
your stooped years were wise

I wish for a moment
to watch your delight
blowing out candles
one breath at a time

I know you were weary
while your soft heart bore all
I think of you daily,
long for your call

I picked beans this morning
from the earth you loved
and our apples are growing
near the cottage for Mom

But the best I can hope for
is a tear in my eye
while time rushes onward
with a breath and a sigh

❖

Lingering late on a summer shore

the sliver of moon a darkened orange
Fading light brings deep calm
where nature can abound

Bats take flight to feast on bugs,
swoop and feed as we watch,
soothed by care and a friendly smile
In the silence a hawk takes wing

delighting us with his princely catch,
a fish alive within his grasp
Burdened by his prize, he flies above us
once then twice again

I sit beside you, feet in the sand
and ask what I don't know
It's been so long since friendship felt new
What are we to learn?

The waves remind me we're not alone,
there are lights on a distant shore
Feeling enraptured with promise
I am careful to take in your tender tone

Dark closes in exposing stars
that shine forever on
I see the soul you seek to be—
a woman bound set free

Free in the love that God has given
to those who are His own
Life is messy and sure to be
'til all are safely home

❖

Swiss Mug

I look for you
in the morning
standing near the sink,
placed there last night
emptied and cooled

Your bold red coat
is easy to spot,
your white cross, your
tea stained center

The sight of you
takes me back
to our first meeting
in Le Gruyere

You, my prized purchase,
replaced the one before—
shelved like a dying friend
I could no longer hold

Now your bright beauty
cheers me each morning,
accepting, holding
boiling contents

Inviting me
to sip slowly,
warming my hands,
warming my heart

❖

All poetry...

is about ducks or geese
Web footed, thick-skinned—
water off a duck's back kind of skin

White with purity,
except when not
Walking in the poop of others
without thought about how it smells
or stays with you

You carry it on your feet into the next experience
accidentally, in your search
for something that feeds you

Poetry is about being alive,
shameless about your waddle
and the magic of taking flight at anything scary

Once in the air
you have perspective
seeing new places to nourish
Or return feet first into favorite waters
with a splash that breaks the silence

You announce yourself in poetry
Quacks and honks harmonizing
with smooth-skinned frogs waiting in the lilies
Searching for the perfect chin thrusted mate

All poetry rises like mist in the morning
Some will see it, only some will catch it—
as fleeting and magnificent as it is

❖

Today I Wish For You

Do you know how much I think of you?
Head down grinding
without the satisfaction of swallow—
this bite too big for even you to chew

I see your face crushed by stress
and a wish that time would pass more quickly

But I remember you with your back on the sofa cushions,
feet stretched toward the ceiling,
book in hand,
devouring the words of a creative genius
Your brain too smart to squander

Your fire, your will and determination
would carry you into halls of learning—
thoughts of serious matters plaguing your happy

Today I wish for you
bare feet on grass,
burdens thrown off—
can we reflect on all you've accomplished
once again with your head in my lap
while we share a song you loved me to sing?

Not one moment wasted
as you churn in the waves
I am your lighthouse—
a forever beacon of the warm fire of home

❖

She is Burning and I Cry

for the Columbia Gorge, 2017

She would say *it's only surface*
and for me, it was time —
my elevation hasn't lessened,
my forest coat was just too tight

And all the people —
so many people!
It never did seem right
to carry all their baggage,
to mend the constant fight

Trains and dams,
tribes and friends,
ships to carry burdens —
Old and new passing through
endless miles of highway

Remember I'm forever
Life will return anew
Beauty rises from the ash
A wasteland doesn't last

So see the beauty in the glow
reflected on the water
Be grateful for my memories

Be kind to little brother
who from his fist a spark did fly,
would turn back time
if he could try

Ignited, united, sorrow

❖

Beauty

has come to her over years of heartache
She has learned to love her children
more as an old woman
then she knew how to in her prime

Love from drooping breasts
and the soft arc of her back
She gets it now—
has renewed purpose in life

Beauty is more than babies—
but the raising of them
nourishing them
through divorce and heartbreak

Beauty walks softly
over warmed tiles
laid down by children
feeling comfort even in their absence

These years of living
long years of the lucky
where enough time
has paved the way to no regrets

Beauty opens her arms
for one more hug
while the heart is still beating
This warmth a treasure
I didn't know I'd collect

Beauty tugs at my heartstrings
while autumn leaves are falling
Winter will find us
wrapped in blankets of thankfulness

❖

A day

of remembrance—
tattered sacred pages,
a single place of solace
for his fearful heart

Words of comfort and inspiration
inked on narrow lines
inside the black leather cover
his hands opened often

Blowing separate thin pages
pure and precious words
available and extraordinary
reveal life to babes

A remnant of personal effects
rests on my bookshelf

We never stop loving a father,
we never forget his skin

So in the warmth of autumn,
let me see the colors passing
cleansed by falling rain
that mutes the tides of change

❖

In my kitchen

she is the beaters
churning, blending
melding all the voices
and ingredients of friendships—
integrating wisdom from experience to experience

She is the meat thermometer
testing, waiting
announcing in perfect timing
when to gather and partake

She is the spatula
enfolding, coaxing in the rebel edges
mixing and transforming my heart batter
prepared to be something beautiful

She is the stainless steel cookware
holding hot brewing emotions to a boiling point
ready to soften hard things
or stiffen the gooey yolks of misunderstanding

She is the metal cookie sheet
willing for the heat
who raises dough into morsels of goodness
then gives up the goods
only to be cooled, washed and sent to a dark place again

She is the timer set and faithful
persistent and loud
taking her job seriously every time

She is the Daphne sprig
removed from the others
set in water at the kitchen window
determined to grow enough roots for transplant
someday
she grows more leaves
even though no one notices
because she loves the sound of voices
and the scent of spices coming from the stove

She is all of you, and she is me

❖

Almost Christmas

Passing, like sunlight in winter,
another decade closing
Our parents stooped, uncertain
Time revealing a final story

Arm in arm we come together
Your eyes softer, wiser, tender
Can we be what we still yearn for?
Kindness is the answer

For you I am grateful
as we walk each other home,
sharing joys and revelation
but sorrows, too, in open arms

❖

There are stories

we hide behind
Distractions
like needy dogs
Persistent

stories
we tell ourselves
to secure our place
last in line

The noise of imagination
drowning out reality

Step up, step out, be seen
she said

❖

Crone Line

I crossed the crone line like a winner—
arms raised and panting
It's where I got my second wind
and made my way more slowly,
stopping often to inspect the words I had chosen
and the lives they touched

Heart pounding in a rhythm
comfortably familiar
I am alive!
I am well, and nothing beats that!

I crossed the crone line
not knowing how much it would mean to me
Skin worn well,
more freckled in sunshine,
grasping the help of women
already over the line

My need for reassurance muted
by a cease from striving
I can lay down with the wolf now
Rest on her furry flank
Feed her nourishing bits of vermin
caught before they get to me

I crossed the crone line and enjoy the view

❖

They say the sky is falling

I can feel it closing in
I look to the birds for guidance
still simply singing their sweet songs

Fear not! the Good Book says,
all this must come to pass
How do I release what's only borrowed
while He slowly folds it up?

The news we get is bad
Science screaming Chicken Little
while the greedy want more time
to rape and pillage what is sacred—
Mother Earth's forgiving heart

The mirror says that we are foolish,
nothing stays around for long
Every power has its downfall,
every man his reckoning

I feel alone just like the others,
trapped inside a cell phone screen
feasting on a stream of sewerage,
too entranced to pull away

What I need is found in quiet
God alone can satisfy
Rest of soul and thankful living
like the birds who hold the sky

Acknowledgments

This book would not have been possible without the kind eyes, intuition and patience of my editor Ash Good. The cover is of my childhood driveway in Paso Robles, California, painted by Brenda Walther. Author portrait by Brian Geraths.

Rhonda Elizabeth Nichols lives in Tigard, Oregon with her husband and her mother resides in a house on their property. She works as a personal companion to those with profound memory loss. She has eleven siblings and spent her early years in the Central Coast of California and her adolescence in southern Oregon. Rhonda discovered her poetic voice in motherhood. Other poems can be found in the anthologies *Poems of July 2013* and *High Priestesses of Poetry.*

CPSIA information can be obtained
at www.ICGtesting.com
Printed in the USA
BVHW090135261120
594139BV00004B/17